Short Stories for Students, Volume 20

Project Editor: Ira Mark Milne

Editorial: Anne Marie Hacht, Michelle Kazensky, Jennifer Smith **Rights Acquisition and Management**: Edna Hedblad, Emma Hull, Sheila Spencer **Manufacturing**: Rhonda Williams

Imaging and Multimedia: Lezlie Light, Mike Logusz, Kelly A. Quin **Product Design**: Pamela A. E. Galbreath

© 2005 Thomson Gale, a part of The Thomson Corporation.

Thomson and Star Logo are trademarks and Gale is a registered trakemark used herein under license.

For more information, contact
Thomson Gale
27500 Drake Rd.
Farmington Hills, MI 48331-3535
Or you can visit our Internet site at

http://www.gale.com **ALL RIGHTS RESERVED**
No part of this work covered by the copyright hereon may be reproduced or used in any form or by any means—graphic, electronic, or mechanical, including photocopying, recording, taping, Web distribution, or information storage retrieval systems—without the written permission of the publisher.

For permission to use material from this product, submit your request via Web at http://www.gale-edit.com/permissions, or you may download our Permissions Request form and submit your request by fax or mail to: *Permissions Department*
Thomson Gale
27500 Drake Rd.
Farmington Hills, MI 48331-3535
Permissions Hotline: 248-699-8006 or 800-877-4253, ext. 8006
Fax: 248-699-8074 or 800-762-4058

Since this page cannot legibly accommodate all copyright notices, the acknowledgments constitute an extension of the copyright notice.

While every effort has been made to ensure the reliability of the information presented in this publication, Thomson Gale does not guarantee the accuracy of the data contained herein. Thomson Gale accepts no payment for listing; and inclusion in the publication of any organization, agency, institution, publication, service, or individual does not imply endorsement of the editors or publisher. Errors brought to the attention of the publisher and verified to the satisfaction of the publisher will be corrected in future editions.

ISBN 0-7876-4272-X
ISSN 1092-7735

Printed in the United States of America
10 9 8 7 6 5 4 3 2 1

Babette's Feast

Isak Dinesen 1950

Introduction

Perhaps best known for *Out of Africa* (1937), Isak Dinesen is the pseudonym of Karen Blixen. Having established her reputation as an author in the 1930s and 1940s, she sought to increase her income in the 1950s by having stories published in American magazines. A number of her stories were featured in *Ladies' Home Journal*, including "Babette's Feast," which was first published in 1950. A friend had advised her to write about food because Americans love food, so she crafted a story about the transformative powers of a very special feast. In 1958, "Babette's Feast," along with other stories published in magazines, was compiled into *Anecdotes of Destiny*, which was available as of

2004.

As a child, Dinesen suffered the loss of her father by suicide. In the wake of this tragedy, her grandmother and a nearby aunt helped care for the family. Through this experience, Dinesen came to understand and appreciate the ways women take care of loved ones and of each other. As an adult, Dinesen found herself operating a coffee farm in East Africa, an experience that taught her a great deal about contrasting people and cultures. Dinesen's admirers and scholars often seek parallels between her life and her writing, and in "Babette's Feast" Dinesen seems to draw on her childhood and adult experiences to give the story depth and authenticity.

Author Biography

Karen Blixen (also known as Isak Dinesen) was born Karen Christentze Dinesen on April 17, 1885, near Copenhagen, Denmark. Her father was loosely related to royalty, and her mother was the daughter of a successful shipowner. When Dinesen was ten, her father committed suicide. This was devastating to Dinesen, who had shared a close relationship with her father.

Literature played a prominent role in Dinesen's family; her grandfather had been friends with the fairy tale author Hans Christian Andersen, and her father, brother, a sister, and an aunt were all writers. When Dinesen was twenty-two, several of her short stories were published in literary journals.

On January 14, 1914, Dinesen married her second cousin, Bror von Blixen-Finecke, a baron's son. With the emotional and financial support of their family, the couple bought 700 acres of land in East Africa and began cultivating it for coffee beans. Within the year, however, Dinesen discovered that she had contracted syphilis from her unfaithful husband. Afraid and angry, she returned to Denmark for treatment. She stayed there for most of 1915 and 1916 before reconciling with Bror. With big dreams, they purchased two more coffee farms, but a series of droughts left them profitless.

Dinesen and Bror separated and then divorced in 1925, leaving Dinesen in charge of the failing coffee farms. Her personal life was further complicated by her romance with a longtime friend, an Englishman named Denys Finch Hatton. She had two miscarriages over the course of their relationship, and he had no intention of marrying her. Dinesen's coffee career ended because of a failed loan, fallen coffee and land prices, locusts, and droughts. In 1931, she sold everything to a local developer. A few weeks later, Hatton died when his small airplane crashed.

Prior to leaving Africa and again after returning to Denmark, Dinesen submitted stories to an American publisher (under the name Isak Dinesen). In 1934, her first book of short stories, *Seven Gothic Tales* was published in America. Critical reception was overwhelmingly positive, although the book failed to make waves in Denmark. When *Out of Africa* was published in 1937, American readers and critics alike applauded the author's work. This time, her Danish readership was equally impressed.

In 1959, Dinesen's health was on the decline. Still, she visited America on a four-month tour, where she was toasted by the elite of New York City, including Pearl S. Buck, e. e. cummings, and Marilyn Monroe. After her return to Denmark, her health continued to deteriorate. On September 7, 1962, she died of malnutrition near Copenhagen.

Plot Summary

Part 1: Two Ladies of Berlevaag

In the town of Berlevaag lived an old man and his two daughters, Martine and Philippa. Martine had been named for Martin Luther, and Philippa (one year younger) had been named for Luther's friend Philip Melanchton. The man, called the Dean, was the leader of a small Lutheran religious sect with a faithful following in the small town. He and his daughters led a puritanical life, and the daughters were expected to forego marriage for the sake of leading the sect after the Dean's death.

After the Dean died, the sisters continued his legacy, keeping the church going and ministering to the poor. Now, many years later, the aging churchgoers are bickering and bringing up past wrongs.

Part 2: Martine's Lover

As young women, Martine and Philippa had been strikingly beautiful. At the age of eighteen, Martine caught the eye of a young lieutenant, Lorens Loewenhielm, who then began visiting the Dean in order to see Martine. Despite his frequent visits, he could never manage to tell her of his feelings for her. Being around her made him feel small and worthless, so on his last visit he boldly kissed her hand and declared that he would never see her again. After this he resolved to forget about her and focus on becoming a great military leader so he would never feel small again.

Part 3: Philippa's Lover

A year later, when Philippa was eighteen, a visiting opera singer from France heard her sing at church. The singer, Achille Papin, was renowned in Paris and was convinced that young Philippa could be the toast of Paris with her exquisite soprano voice. The Dean agreed to allow Papin to give the girl lessons, but when Papin rehearsed a romantic duet with her, he kissed her. She returned home and asked her father to write a letter telling Papin she would no longer accept instruction from him. Papin felt a deep loss for the world of music, and he barely remembered the kiss.

Part 4: A Letter from Paris

Fifteen years later, a ragged-looking woman appears on the sisters' doorstep with a letter from Papin. He explains that this woman, Babette Hersant, has fled Paris for her life. He hopes that Martine and Philippa will be kind enough to take her in as a maid, as she has nowhere else to go, having lost her husband and son in an uprising. Babette assures the sisters that she will work as their maid and cook for nothing, and the sisters agree to the arrangement.

Part 5: Still Life

At first, the sisters are wary of their new maid. She speaks only French, looks like a beggar, and is Catholic. As they get accustomed to her, however, they realize that she is strong and kind and has their best interests at heart. Although Papin's letter informed the sisters that Babette could cook, they show her how to prepare the plain dishes to which they are accustomed. Gradually, the sisters' affection for her grows, as does the affection of the members of the church. Martine and Philippa realize, however, that there is much about Babette that they do not know and that she holds painful secrets from her past.

Part 6: Babette's Good Luck

For years, Babette had continued to play the French lottery by mail. As luck would have it, she won the ten-thousand-franc prize just as the sisters were trying to plan a celebration of what would have been their father's hundredth birthday. Babette asked that they allow her to pay for and prepare an authentic French meal for the sisters and their guests. They are nervous about the dishes that will be served, and they are hesitant to accept Babette's generous offer to pay. The sisters reluctantly agree.

Part 7: The Turtle

Babette leaves for ten days to make arrangements for the ingredients for the dinner.

Upon her return, Martine and Philippa notice that Babette is particularly bright and enthusiastic in anticipation of the meal. A few weeks later, strange bottles, ingredients (including a large turtle), and other items begin arriving at the house. The sisters become anxious about their guests' response to the foreign dishes, and they appeal to their guests to be as gracious as possible because they are only allowing this meal out of kindness to their servant. The church members, who love Martine and Philippa, gladly agree.

Part 8: The Hymn

The morning of the celebration, Martine and Philippa receive a note that Mrs. Loewenhielm will be bringing her nephew, General Loewenhielm, with her that evening. The General recalls his awkward appearances there as a young lieutenant and looks forward to the chance to show more poise and confidence this time. Martine and Philippa inform Babette that there will be one more for dinner and that it is a man who spent several years in Paris. Babette is delighted.

When the guests arrive, they join hands and begin singing the Dean's favorite hymns. It is a time of sharing and community, and when they sit down to the meal, they are beginning to feel more unified than they have in years.

Part 9: General Loewenhielm

On the drive to the dinner, Loewenhielm had been reflecting on his life and the fact that, despite his military glory, earthly success, and beautiful wife, he is basically unhappy. He had begun to worry about the state of his soul but lacked direction on how to resolve his angst. He remembered the brash young officer he had been years before and how he had dreamed of having everything he now has.

Part 10: Babette's Dinner

A member of the congregation says the blessing over the meal, and Babette's hired assistant begins serving the food and wine. With each course, Loewenhielm is more amazed at how fine the food is and how it reminds him of his days at Paris's finest restaurants. Meanwhile, the conversation at the table revolves around miracles they had all seen during the Dean's years of ministry.

Part 11: General Loewenhielm's Speech

Overcome by the experience of the meal and the feeling of hospitality, Loewenhielm stands up to deliver a speech about righteousness and bliss. He is so eloquent that even though his fellow guests do not understand everything he says, they are moved. Around the table, the men and women of the congregation make amends for their recent bickering and grudges.

As the guests prepare to return home, the sisters walk them to the door. Before leaving, Loewenhielm confesses to Martine that he has never forgotten her and that he never will. They part amicably.

Part 12: The Great Artist

With the meal concluded, Martine and Philippa go to the kitchen to find Babette. She is surrounded by piles of dirty dishes and pots. They thank her for such a fine meal and for all of her work. She admits that she was once the chef at one of Paris's finest restaurants, but when the sisters ask about her return to Paris now that she has money, she answers that she will never go back to Paris. The sisters are relieved but surprised. Babette explains that she prepared the meal that night for herself because she is a great artist and needed to express her artistry. Back in Paris, the life she knew and the people who appreciated her work are all gone. She also tells them that she cannot return to Paris because she has spent her entire lottery winnings on this one meal.

With the understanding of who Babette truly is and how she sees herself, the sisters are moved to compassion. Philippa embraces her and assures her that her art is not lost, because in paradise she will be all God meant her to be.

Characters

Babette Hersant

Babette is welcomed into the home of Martine and Philippa because she is in dire need of a place to stay. She has fled Paris after she and her husband and son participated in an uprising and her two men were killed. Under accusations of arson, she left the country to save her life, taking with her a letter from Achille Papin asking the sisters to take Babette into their home.

Babette is confident, frugal, intelligent, congenial, loyal, and hardworking. She treats the sisters with respect and devotion, despite the many differences between them and herself. Although the sisters do not know it until the end, Babette had been a renowned Parisian chef. This is part of her identity, as she considers herself a great artist who must express her art in order to feel fulfilled. She waits patiently for twelve years before being given the opportunity to prepare a lavish meal for the sisters, an experience that means more to her than it does to them.

Lorens Loewenhielm

When the reader first meets Loewenhielm, he is a young lieutenant in the military, who is smitten with Martine. Never able to bring himself to reveal his feelings for her, he determines to continue his military career and be great so that he will not feel the awkwardness and unworthiness he felt around Martine. Many years later at the dinner, he is a guest. Having become a general with numerous achievements and medals, he feels self-confident entering the house that had intimidated him as a young man. At the same time, he has become introspective in his older age, and he realizes that all the "trappings" of the good life he pursued have failed to make him truly happy.

Martine

Martine is the slightly older sister in the story. As a young woman, her beauty had caught the attention of many men (including Lieutenant Loewenhielm), but she remained loyal to her father's church and his expectation that she and Philippa would oversee it after his death. As a result, she never marries, and she and her sister live together throughout their lives.

Martine is devout, kind, and non-judgmental. She honors her father's memory and loves her sister. Martine and her sister have led sheltered lives, and they both resist change. Martine's anxiety regarding the unknown is evident in the episode in which she sees the large turtle brought in for Babette's meal and is so terrified she has nightmares. Still, she decides that Babette's feelings are more important than her own anxiety. She visits the men and women of the congregation who will be guests at the dinner, asking them to pretend to enjoy the meal, even if the dishes served are very strange. This gesture demonstrates her sensitivity to the feelings of others.

Achille Papin

A great French opera singer, Achille Papin takes a leisure trip to Norway, where he meets eighteen-year-old Philippa. Her voice astounds him, and he arranges to give her private voice lessons. During a duet, however, he kisses her, and she ends the lessons. Though he is disappointed not to see Philippa again, he is more distraught over what the world of art has lost in Philippa's decision not to pursue singing.

Papin is basically a kindhearted man who enjoys his fame and the benefits it brings him. The reader sees how his compassion has grown over the years when he comes to Babette's aid in Paris. With her life at risk, he remembers the two gentle Norwegian sisters and sends Babette to them with a personal letter asking them to care for her.

Philippa

One year younger than Martine, Philippa is the other daughter of the Dean. Together, she and her sister oversee their father's Lutheran sect in their small hometown. Like her sister, she honors her father's desire that they focus on the congregation rather than marry and have their own families. Also like her sister, she seems to bear no resentment for this course in life, and she and Martine live happily together for their entire lives.

Philippa has a beautiful voice, and in her youth it captured the attention of the French opera singer, Achille Papin. She turns from pursuing developing this talent, however, and devotes her life to her father's congregation. Philippa is a kind and religious woman who leads a plain but satisfying life. Her sensitivity is demonstrated in the last scene when, after Babette has revealed her identity as a chef and an artist, Philippa embraces her and encourages her in her art. She assures Babette that her days as an artist are not over because in heaven she will enjoy the fullness of her art as it was meant to be.

Themes

Food

The predominant theme of "Babette's Feast" is how food can transform the hearts of people and the atmosphere of a gathering. Prior to Babette's appearance on their doorstep, Martine and Philippa regarded food as something plain that had the sole purpose of providing their necessary sustenance. Because their lifestyle requires shunning the pleasures of the flesh, they had never considered food a luxurious experience to be enjoyed. Babette, on the other hand, has a very different perspective; she adores preparing exquisite food to delight others, and when she is finally given the chance to do this for the sisters and their congregation, the story takes on new life. The meal she prepares creates an atmosphere that fosters interaction and delight. Dinesen explains: "Usually in Berlevaag people did not speak much while they were eating. But somehow this evening tongues were loosened." She adds:

> Most often the people in Berlevaag during the course of a good meal would come to feel a little heavy. Tonight it was not so. The *convives* grew lighter in weight and lighter of heart the more they ate and drank. They no longer needed to remind

themselves of their vow [to pretend to enjoy the meal despite the strange dishes]. It was, they realized, when man has not only altogether forgotten but has firmly renounced all ideas of food and drink that he eats and drinks in the right spirit.

Media Adaptations

- In 1987, Danish writer and director Gabriel Axel adapted "Babette's Feast" to film for Orion Pictures. It garnered an impressive following and won the 1988 Academy Award for Best Foreign Film.

Even before the feast, Dinesen reveals that Babette has unusual powers with food. When she takes over running the house for the sisters, she respects their work feeding the needy. The sisters notice that "the soup-pails and baskets acquired a new, mysterious power to stimulate and strengthen their poor and sick." Whether she is cooking for friends, hostesses, strangers, the needy, or the wealthy, Babette has a special gift with food that fulfills her while satisfying others.

Contrast

Throughout the story, Dinesen sets up a variety of contrasts. Most of the contrast is between Babette and her hostesses, Martine and Philippa. Babette is an entirely different kind of woman than they are, and Dinesen draws these lines very clearly. Whereas Babette is dark, the sisters are fair. Whereas Babette is a French Catholic fleeing danger and unrest, the sisters are Norwegian Lutherans secure in their familiar and predictable environment. Whereas Babette embraces worldly experience and pleasure (though not to excess), the sisters consciously avoid such things. The religious contrast is an important one to the sisters, a lesson they learned from their father, who upon learning that Papin was Roman Catholic "grew a little pale," as he had never actually seen a Roman Catholic in person. Dinesen writes that the sisters and their congregation "renounced the pleasures of this world, for the earth and all that it held to them was but a kind of illusion." Shedding light on the sisters' upbringing, Dinesen offers a contrast between them and the world beyond the environment created by their father; the sisters are described as having had an "almost supernatural fairness of flowering fruit trees or perpetual snow," and they "did not let themselves be touched by the flames of this world." On the evening of the dinner, Babette's diligent and frantic preparations in the kitchen contrast sharply with the sisters' preparation for the event. Martine and Philippa "put on their old black best frocks and their confirmation gold crosses. They sat down, folded their hands in their laps and committed themselves unto God."

Topics for Further Study

- After so many years of living a certain way, Babette reveals much about herself to Martine and Philippa at the feast. Given the ways the characters interacted during the feast, how do you think the women's relationships may be different afterwards? How may they remain the same? Do you think Babette continues to live with the sisters? Write an "Afterword" addressing these questions. You may write it in Dinesen's style or approach it as an objective follow-up.

- Imagine that you are in a similar position as Babette after she won the money and offered to prepare an authentic French meal. Consider your own family's background, and prepare a menu for a feast featuring dishes from the native land of part or all of your family. Include at least three recipes with the menu. Be sure to consider every course of the meal and include beverages.

- Research the Evangelical Lutheran Church of Norway. If you have difficulty finding enough information, extend your research to other Scan-dinavian Lutheran churches. How has it changed since the eighteenth and nineteenth centuries? Were sects like that formed by the Dean common, and what kinds of factors led groups to differentiate themselves slightly from the main church body?

- Babette considers herself a great artist because she is a great chef. Do you agree that cuisine is a form of art? In the story, what does her cooking have in common with other forms of art, and how is it different? Choose one other student in the class whose opinion differs from yours and hold an informal debate with a panel of three students who will decide which of you makes the stronger arguments.

What makes the idea of contrast a theme rather than a stylistic consideration is what Dinesen does with it. Rather than use it as a way to generate interest in the characters, she brings all the contrasts between Babette and the sisters to the moment of the feast, where she demonstrates how their differences ultimately bring them closer together. To everyone's surprise, their differences are not irreconcilable, as General Loewenhielm announces in his toast, "Righteousness and bliss have kissed one another!" By treating each other with kindness and understanding, the women learn that their differences in no way prevent them from achieving emotional intimacy. This closeness is hinted at earlier in the story, when the sisters have taken Babette into their home and are getting to know her better. Dinesen reveals a realization they make: "She had appeared to be a beggar; she turned out to be a conqueror." The contrast between the first impression she made and the person she actually is only important because the sisters keep their hearts open to finding out who Babette really is.

Style

Biblical Allusion

Biblically well-read, Dinesen applies her knowledge of Scripture in "Babette's Feast" to underscore the strong religious overtones of Martine and Philippa's home they share with Babette. Throughout the story, subtle biblical allusions are introduced without reference, giving them the natural context of everyday thought that they have in the hearts of the sisters and the congregation. In describing the sisters' beauty in their youth, Dinesen explains that they caught the eyes of the men in the congregation. She writes that the older men "had been prizing the maidens far above rubies," an allusion to Proverbs 3:15 ("She is more precious than rubies; nothing you desire can compare to her") and Proverbs 31:10 ("A wife of noble character who can find? She is worth far more than rubies").

Babette is also the subject of biblical allusions. At one point, she is likened to Martha and the sisters to Mary, a reference to a story in the book of Luke (Luke 10:38–42) in which Jesus visits the sisters Mary and Martha. While Martha busies herself with hostess duties and preparing food, Mary sits quietly to learn. Babette is also deemed a "good and faithful servant," an allusion to the parable of the talents. In this parable, a master puts some of his servants in charge of money to see what they do with it. The servant who doubles his sum is praised, "Well done, good and faithful servant!" (Matthew 25:21).

The feast itself inspires a reference to the wedding in which Jesus turned water into wine (John 2:1–11). Dinesen writes, "They were sitting down to a meal, well, so had people done at the wedding of Cana. And grace has chosen to manifest itself there, in the very wine, as fully as anywhere." This is a significant reference for the conservative Lutherans at the meal because it gives them biblical permission to enjoy the event and its wine, and it is the first step toward the eventual reconciliation of the pleasures of the world and the fullness of the spirit.

Simile

Perhaps because the Norwegian setting and characters were unfamiliar to her American readers ("Babette's Feast" was, after all, written for an American magazine), Dinesen scatters similes throughout her story to provide her readers with familiar images. This approach begins in the very first paragraph, where Dinesen writes of the small town of Berlevaag that it "looks like a child's toy-town of little wooden pieces painted gray, tallow, pink and many other colors." When Babette asks if she may use her lottery winnings to pay for and prepare a lavish French meal, Dinesen writes, "Babette's dark eyes were as eager and pleading as a dog's." General Loewenhielm dresses in his military regalia for the feast, and when he arrives, "in his bright uniform, his breast covered with decorations, [he] strutted and shone like an ornamental bird. A golden pheasant or a peacock, in this sedate party of black crows and jackdaws."

Historical Context

Norway in the 1870s

In the 1870s, Norway was a relatively peaceful, prosperous nation. Although it was under Swedish rule, Norway had been allowed to have its own constitution. This simply meant that rather than being governed by its own monarch, it was under the authority of Sweden. In the Parliament and among the people, however, a growing nationalist movement began to pave the way for Norway's eventual independence. Economically, Norway was healthy. Increased trade and more favorable tariffs brought Norway further into the opportunities offered by the European economy. Modernity was making its way into the country's business and daily life: The first railway had been in operation since 1854, the telegraph was available, and agricultural methods had been modernized. Industry had grown substantially since the 1840s, which, combined with the increased trade, substantially grew the merchant fleet.

With the economic upturns, however, came class conflict and a call for social reforms. This eventually led to the first liberal political block that challenged the predominant conservative thinkers in government. Still, it would not be until 1884 that this block would officially become a political party.

Compare & Contrast

- **1870s:** Although Norway has its own constitution and its Parliament is growing stronger, it is under Swedish rule. This and other factors feed a rising nationalism that results in Norway's independence in 1905.

  1950s: Having regained its independence, Norway returns to its government structure of a constitutional monarchy. Norway has deserted its World War I neutrality and joined NATO, making it a more active player in international affairs.

  Today: In the 1990s, Norway maintains its independence from the European Union. The 1994 vote is very close, with a slight majority of 52 percent voting against joining Europe.

- **1870s:** The state church is still the Evangelical Lutheran Church of Norway. Put in place after the Reformation in 1500, the state church is funded by the government. Most Norwegians are members of this church. Having a state church does not, however, prohibit free practice of other faiths and denominations.

1950s: Little has changed over the years. The Evangelical Lutheran Church of Norway is still the state church, and most Norwegians continue to be members with varying degrees of activity.

Today: Approximately 90 percent of Norwegians are affiliated with the Evangelical Lutheran Church of Norway. While it is still the state church, a growing number of Norwegians favor separating the church and the government.

- **1870s:** About thirty years after Norway began to establish industrial businesses, such as textile factories, the economy is healthy and strong. During this period, the number of merchant ships in Norway rises substantially, evidence of the growth of Norway's industries.

  1950s: In the post–World War II years, Norway's economy has grown. More attention is given to building welfare programs to provide for the low-income segments of the population.

  Today: As a result of the strong economy and the postwar welfare programs, Norwegian society is less characterized by class distinctions than many Western nations.

- **1870s:** Women are second to men in Norwegian society. Although they won inheritance rights in the 1850s, women are still barred from pursuing higher education, and married women are not allowed to manage money.

  1950s: Progress in women's rights has been made, but inequality still characterizes gender rights and privileges. With the rise of industrialism, more women have entered the workforce, but at lower pay rates than men receive. Women also have the right to vote.

  Today: Women hold visible positions in government and occupy numerous seats in the Parliament. Women comprise at least half of all college graduates each year, and the government has handed down "affirmative action"–type statutes to increase the number of women in the workforce.

The population in 1870s Norway was quite homogenous. There were very few non-Norwegians, so the language and customs of Norway remained well preserved. Family life was very traditional, with women expected to marry young, have children, and maintain the home, whereas men were expected to work hard to provide for their families.

The 1871 Communard Uprising in Paris

France in the mid-nineteenth century was a place of political turmoil. Between 1852 and 1871, the period called the Second Empire saw the Emperor Napoleon III pursue colonial expansion and foster a strong economy. The Franco-Prussian War, however, lasted from 1870 to 1871 and brought France and its emperor to its knees. A provisional government was put in place as a stopgap until February 1871, when elections were held for a National Assembly. A group of radicals, however, were angry at how quickly France had surrendered to Prussia and how the new government was shaping up to be conservative. In March, these radicals and the National Guard seized Paris and appointed themselves the *Communards* (supporters of *La Commune de Paris*) to take over as the governing body. Government troops were sent on May 21 to destroy the *Communards*, and the week that followed became known as "Bloody Week." After the defeat, punishments were handed down to those who participated. In all, eighteen thousand Parisians lost their lives and seven thousand were deported.

Critical Overview

Critics generally characterize "Babette's Feast" as a triumphant and sensitive story of generosity, grace, and healing. John Simon of *National Review* deems it as "one of the author's finest." The characterization of the women in the story and the relationships between them strike readers as believable and sympathetic. In the *New Republic*, Stanley Kauffmann observed, "Lightly but clearly interwoven in the story are oppositions of cultures —pleasure-loving Catholic France, dour and hell-conscious Protestant Denmark." Despite the differences between Babette and the sisters Martine and Philippa, the women find a way to live contentedly together, caring for each other and finally getting to know each other in meaningful ways. In fact, Bruce Bassoff of *Studies in Short Fiction* notes that "Babette's Feast" features new knowledge and "a desire for transcendence," which are present in other short stories by Dinesen. Her use of these ideas and plot elements in multiple stories suggests that depicting them to her readers was important to Dinesen.

Dinesen's use of food in the story is a frequent topic of critical discussion. Dinesen uses food in the story in two opposing ways: first as an outward reflection of the differences between Babette and her hostesses and then as a means of bringing unity and commonality to a diverse group of people. In *Style*, critic Esther Rashkin comments on the former:

> Food has tended to be viewed allegorically in the story as representing, for example, the schism between the ethical, Norwegian, puritanical sect of Protestantism, nurtured on split cod and ale-and-bread soup, and the aesthetic, sensuous inclinations of French Catholicism, nourished by haute cuisine and epitomized by the master chef Babette.

She adds:

> There is no denying that Babette's sumptuous feast and its aftermath offer a reflection on religion and on the opposition between the spiritual and the carnal, while also raising questions of artistic creation and identity.

More attention, however, is given to the banquet that gives the story its title. With the feast itself, Dinesen not only introduces the sense of sharing that comes with enjoying a meal together, but she adds the elements of generosity, service, mystery, and revelation. Rashkin notes that the feast demonstrates how the differences between Babette and the sisters come together in a unique and transformative way over the course of the evening. Of particular interest to Rashkin is the way the dinner opens up the hearts and mouths of the guests to explore emotional territory previously kept private. She notes that many of the guests, along with the main characters, have suffered loss that remained unspoken until the feast. She explains that the dinner "allows for a communion in loss by enabling loss to be talked about and the process of mourning to begin." Rashkin concludes her commentary by suggesting that writing this story had a similarly cathartic purpose for Dinesen, who endured considerable loss during her years in Africa. Having lost her coffee farms, her husband, her lover, two pregnancies, and almost two decades, she returned to Denmark alone. Rashkin offers this biographical interpretation of "Babette's Feast":

> If Africa was for Dinesen a "child she had buried" and could only talk or write about from a distance, and if "Babette's Feast" is all about the creation of a work of art as the therapeutic medium for "talking" about loss, we may suggest that Dinesen too, like the sisters ... "used" this narrative for her own therapeutic needs.... Created as a symptom of her need to grieve, as a vehicle for facilitating the grieving process, and as a subtle commentary on the intricate relationship between writing and bereavement, "Babette's Feast" can ultimately be read as a text that humorously and poignantly tells the tale of Dinesen's own recipe for mourning.

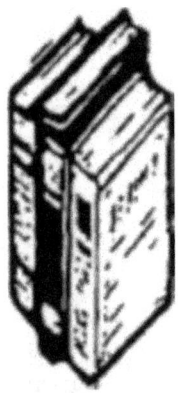

What Do I Read Next?

- All of the short stories in the collection *Anecdotes of Destiny* (1958), including "Babette's Feast," were written by Dinesen in the 1950s for American magazines and American readers.

- Karen Blixen (as Isak Dinesen) is best known for *Out of Africa* (1937). Largely based on her actual experiences in Africa trying to operate successful coffee farms, this book remains popular because of its descriptions of landscape, animals, and people and its honest portrayal of a difficult lifestyle.

- *Like Water for Chocolate* (1992) is Laura Esquivel's magical yet realistic novel about the emotional and spiritual effects food can have. The novel is set in Mexico and tells the story of a young woman forced to allow her sister to marry her lover. Her ability to cook, however, includes the ability to use her emotions and passions as ingredients.

- Einar Molland's *Church Life in Norway: 1800–1950* (1978) closely examines the role of the state church in Norway and its influence on daily life. Molland also explores challenges to the church's theological views over this time span and how these challenges have affected the church's position in Norwegian society.

Sources

Bassoff, Bruce, "Babette Can Cook: Life and Art in Three Stories by Isak Dinesen," in *Studies in Short Fiction*, Vol. 27, No. 3, Summer 1990, pp. 385–89.

Dinesen, Isak, "Babette's Feast," in *Anecdotes of Destiny and Ehrengard*, 1958, reprint, Vintage Books, 1985, pp. 21–68.

Donelson, Linda G., "Karen Blixen," in *Dictionary of Literary Biography*, Vol. 214, *Twentieth-Century Danish Writers*, edited by Marianne Stecher-Hansen, Gale, 1999, pp. 41–59.

Ewbank, Inga-stina, "Isak Dinesen," in *European Writers*, Vol. 10, Charles Scribner's Sons, 1990, pp. 1281–1305.

Kauffmann, Stanley, "Changes of Voice and Place," Review of films *Babette's Feast* and *Distant Harmony*, in *New Republic*, Vol. 198, No. 12, March 21, 1988, pp. 26–27.

"Norway," in *Worldmark Encyclopedia of the Nations*, Gale, 2001.

Norway.org Web site; URL: http://www.norway.org/culture.

The Random House Dictionary, 1967, s.v. "art."

Rashkin, Esther, "A Recipe for Mourning: Isak Dinesen's 'Babette's Feast,'" in *Style*, Vol. 29, No. 3, Fall 1995, pp. 356–74.

Simon, John, "Food for Thought," Review of film *Babette's Feast,* in *National Review*, Vol. 40, No. 8, April 29, 1988, pp. 50–51.

Further Reading

Danielsen, Rolf, Stale Dyrvik, Tore Gronlie, Knut Helie, and Edgar Hovland, *Norway: A History from the Vikings to Our Own Times*, Scandinavian University Press, 1995.

> Beginning with the mysterious Vikings, Danielsen *et al.* take the reader through Norway's intriguing history of thought and culture. These five historians account for Norway's economic, social, and political changes over the years. This volume originally appeared in Norwegian.

Hope, Nicholas, *German and Scandinavian Protestantism: 1700–1918*, Oxford University Press, 1995.

> Hope offers a history of the Lutheran church in Germany and Scandinavia, explaining its roots in the Reformation, its place in society, and its handling of the crisis of World War I.

Pelensky, Olga Anastasia, ed., *Isak Dinesen: Critical Views*, Ohio University Press, 1993.

> With twenty-six articles, this collection of literary criticism provides an overview of the works of Dinesen.

Thurman, Judith, *Isak Dinesen: The Life of a Storyteller*, St. Martin's Press, 1982.

> Regarded by many as one of the best biographies of Dinesen, this book takes the reader from Dinesen's birth and childhood, through her tumultuous years in Africa, to her death in Denmark.

CPSIA information can be obtained
at www.ICGtesting.com
Printed in the USA
BVHW042149270821
615504BV00017B/219